LET'S SING ABOUT AMERICA

Illustrated by
Kevin O'Malley and
Thomas J. Messmer

Troll Associates

LIBRARY OF CONGRESS CATALOGING-IN-PUBLICATION DATA
Let's sing about America / illustrated by Kevin O'Malley and
Thomas J. Messmer.
p. of music. — (Troll singalongs)
For voice and piano, with chord symbols.
Principally arr. by Andrew Belling.
Summary: A collection of traditional American songs, including "On
Top of Old Smoky," "Turkey in the Straw," and "Clementine."
ISBN 0-8167-2982-4 (lib. bdg.)   ISBN 0-8167-2983-2 (pbk.)
1. Children's songs—United States.   2. Folk music— United States.
3. Folk songs, English—United States.   [1. Folk songs—United
States.]   I. O'Malley, Kevin, ill.   II. Messmer, Thomas J., ill.
III. Belling, Andrew.   IV. Series.
M1997.L58   1993   92-763081

Published by Troll Associates
Words and music for "Mississippi Line" by Andrew Belling
Original arrangements for all other titles by Andrew Belling
Text copyright © 1993 Troll Associates
Illustration copyright © 1993 Kevin O'Malley and Thomas J. Messmer
The publisher wishes to thank Randa Kirshbaum for her transcriptions
of these original musical arrangements.

Printed in the United States of America
10 9 8 7 6 5 4 3 2 1

Contents

On Top of Old Smoky

Ballad

Arranged by Andrew Belling

1. On top of Old Smok - y, ... all
2. For court - in's a pleas - ure ... but

cov - ered with snow, ... I lost my true
flirt - in's a grief, ... and a false- heart - ed

lov - er ... from court - in' too
lov - er ... is worse than a

slow.

thief.

4

3. For a thief, he will rob you
   and take what you own,
   but a false-hearted lover
   will leave you alone.

4. He'll hug you and kiss you
   and tell you more lies
   than the leaves in the forest
   or stars in the sky.

5. On top of old Smoky,
   all covered with snow,
   I lost my true lover
   from courtin' too slow.

6. From courtin' too slow, love,
   from courtin' too slow.
   On top of old Smoky
   is where I must go.

Turkey in the Straw

Arranged by Andrew Belling

Hee haw

As— I was walk-in' down a coun-try road with a ti-red team and a heav-y load, I cracked my whip and the lead-er sprung. Says I, "Good-bye," to the wag-on tongue.

Chorus

Tur-key in the straw, tur-key in the straw, roll 'em up, twist 'em up a

high tuck 'em haw, and— hit up a tune called "Tur-key In The Straw."

2. Went out to milk and I didn't know how.
   Milked a goat, instead of a cow.
   A monkey sittin' on a pile of straw,
   winkin' at his mother-in-law.

Chorus

(Modulate to A Maj.)

3. Met a big catfish comin' down the stream.
   Says the big catfish, "What do you mean?"
   Caught the big catfish right on the snout.
   Turned Mr. Catfish inside out.

Chorus, twice

7

Down in the Valley

Arranged by Andrew Belling

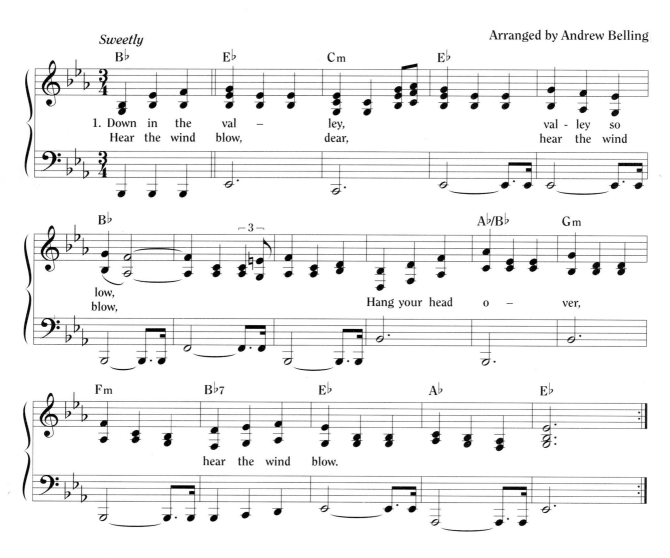

Sweetly

1. Down in the val — ley, val-ley so
Hear the wind blow, dear, hear the wind

low, Hang your head o — ver,
blow,

hear the wind blow.

2. Roses love sunshine, tulips love dew,
   angels in heaven know I love you.
   Know I love you, dear, know I love you.
   Angels in heaven know I love you.

Repeat verse 1

8

John Henry

Arranged by Andrew Belling

Four strong beats

When John Hen-ry was a lit-tle ba-by, when John Hen-ry was a lit-tle boy, all he ev-er want-ed was his dad-dy's ham-mer, and that ham-mer was his fa-vor-ite toy, oh, yes,— that ham-mer was his fa-vor-ite toy.

2. When John Henry married him a woman,
   she would cook him dinner every noon.
   He had ninety miles of track he was gonna have to line.
   Gonna line 'em by the light of the moon, Lord, Lord,
   Gonna line 'em by the light of the moon.

3. Well, the captain said to John Henry,
   "Gonna bring that steam drill 'round.
   Gonna bring that steam drill out here on the line.
   Gonna whup that steel on down, Lord, Lord,…"

4. So John Henry told his captain,
   "Well, a man ain't nothin' but a man.
   And before I let your steam drill beat me down,
   gonna die with the hammer in my hand, Lord, Lord,…"

5. So John Henry took his heavy hammer
   and beside that steam drill stand.
   He was faster than the drill, and he kept on workin' till
   he died with the hammer in his hand, Lord, Lord,…

6. Well, they laid John Henry by the railroad
   and they put him in the sand.
   Now every engine that comes rollin' down the track whistles,
   "There lies a steel drivin' man, Lord, Lord,…"

11

I've Been Working On the Railroad

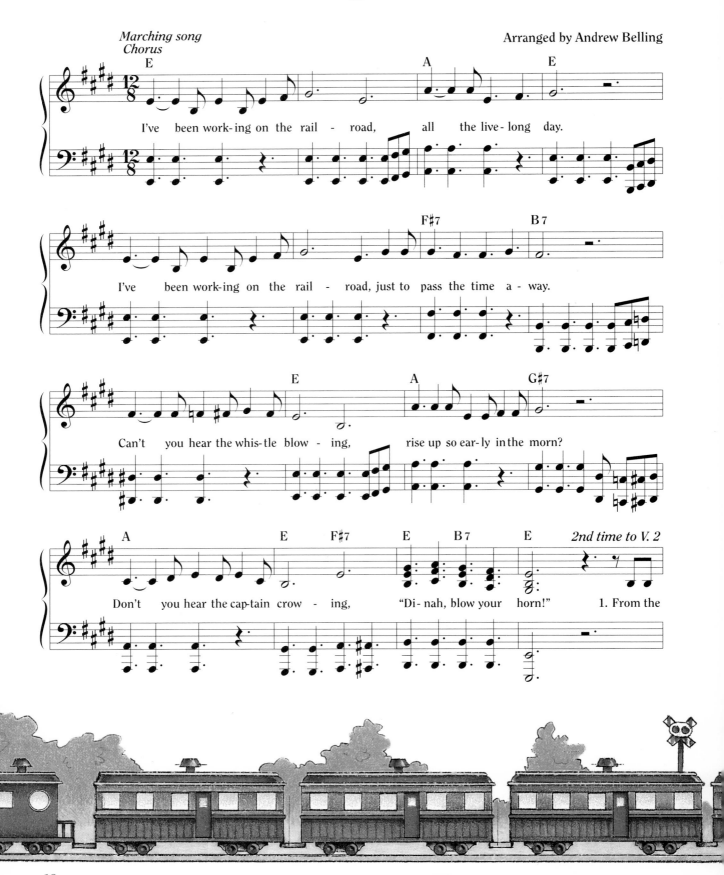

Marching song
Chorus

Arranged by Andrew Belling

I've been work-ing on the rail - road, all the live-long day.

I've been work-ing on the rail - road, just to pass the time a - way.

Can't you hear the whis-tle blow - ing, rise up so ear-ly in the morn?

Don't you hear the cap-tain crow - ing, "Di-nah, blow your horn!"

2nd time to V. 2

1. From the

great At-lan-tic O-cean to the wide Pa-cif-ic's shore, From
2. Lis-ten to the rhy-thm, the rum-ble and the roar. She's

those we left be-hind us to those we'll see once more. She's
steam-ing through the val-leys, up the moun-tains to the shore.

rid-ing tall and hand-some and so well known by all. You can
Hear her bell and whis-tle, a sound that's known by all.

2nd time da Capo

Glid-ing a-cross the coun-try-side, she's the Wa-bash Can-non-ball.
feel the might-y en-gine of the Wa-bash Can-non-ball.

fine

Rock Island Line

Arranged by Andrew Belling

know you're gon - na miss me when I'm gone.

Chorus

2. A-B-C double X-Y-Zee
   The cat's on the cupboard
   and you don't see me.

Chorus

3. Hallelujah, I'm a-safe from sin.
   The good Lord's comin'
   for to see me again.

Chorus

4. Ride by day, ride by night.
   You keep on riding
   till you're out of sight.

Chorus

5. Now this here train has got one design
   to keep on goin'
   till the end of the line.

Chorus

Shortnin' Bread

Skipping song
Chorus, twice

Arranged by Andrew Belling

Chorus, twice

2. Three little babies lyin' in bed.
   Two was sick with a pain in the head.
   Sent for the doctor, the doctor said,
   "Give 'em all a little shortnin' bread."

Chorus, twice

3. Slipped in the kitchen, slipped up the lead,
   slipped my pockets full of shortnin' bread.
   Stole the skillet, stole the lead,
   stole that girl who makes the shortnin' bread.

Chorus, twice

4. Caught with the skillet, caught with the lead,
   caught with the girl makin' shortnin' bread.
   Paid for the skillet, paid for the lead,
   stayed in jail, eatin' shortnin' bread.

Chorus, twice

Clementine

Arranged by Andrew Belling

In a cav - ern, in a can - yon, ex - ca - va - ting for a mine, dwelt a

min - er, for - ty nin - er, and his daugh - ter Cle - men - tine. Oh, my

dar - ling, oh, my dar - ling, oh, my dar - ling Cle - men - tine. You are

gone and lost for - ev - er, dread - ful sor - ry, Cle - men - tine.

2. Light she was and like a feather
   tho' her shoes were number nine.
   Herring boxes without topses,
   sandals were for Clementine.

Chorus

3. Drove her ducklings to the water
   every morning just at nine.
   Hit her foot against a splinter,
   fell into the foamy brine.

Chorus

4. Ruby lips above the water
   blowing bubbles soft and fine,
   but for me, I am no swimmer,
   so I lost my Clementine.

Chorus, twice

Pick a Bale O' Cotton

Arranged by Andrew Belling

2. Me and my brother can pick a bale o' cotton, yes,
   me and my brother can pick a bale a day.
   Me and my brother can pick a bale o' cotton, yes,
   me and my brother can pick a bale a day.

Chorus, twice

Modulate to G Maj.

3. Oh, see my sister pick a bale o'cotton,
   you can see my sister pick a bale a day,...

Chorus, twice

4. Everybody watch me pick a bale o' cotton,
   I say, everybody watch me pick a bale a day,...

Chorus, twice

Repeat verse 1

Chorus, twice

21

Mississippi Line

Words and music by Andrew Belling

Steam - boat's com - in' down the Mis - sis - sip - pi, don't know if it's a -
Shov - el coal in, keep it mov - in', have to reach that one horse

com - in' our way. Load - ed car - go, full of pas - sen - gers, I
town on time. That's the way things have to keep a - go - in'

hope that steam-boat's a - com - in' to stay.
when you trav - el the Mis - sis - sip - pi Line.

Chorus

"Mark Twain" is their cry as they shuf - fle a - long.

2. Steamboat's comin' down the Mississippi,
   Don't know if it's a-comin' our way.
   Down that river from another stop,
   I hope that steamboat's a-comin' today.
   Watch the smoke as she blows from the
     double-stacks
   and see the paddle wheel a-chuggin' around.
   Slip 'n' slide through old Mississippi waters
   hardly even a-makin' a sound.

Chorus
   Steer clear of that land if you want to survive.
   Got to keep awake to keep alive.

3. Steamboat moves no matter what the
     weather is
   and if it rains that's a pretty good sign.
   Means you'll find a golden rainbow waitin'
   at the end of the Mississippi Line.
   You'll find a rainbow at the end of the line!

Erie Canal

Arranged by Andrew Belling

Working song

1. I've— got a mule   and her   name is   Sal.—   Fif - teen   miles   on the
2. Bet- ter move a - long   to - day, old   gal.—

E - rie Ca-nal.—   She's a   good   hard   work er and a   real   good   pal.—
'cause it's   on - ly   me   and my   good mule   Sal.—

Fif - teen   miles   on the   E - rie Ca-nal.—   We've hauled   some barg - es
Git   up,   old gal,   here

in our   day,—   filled   with   lum - ber,   coal   and hay.—   We've
comes a   lock.—   We'll   be   in   town   by   six   o' - clock.

Chorus, twice

Git Along Little Dogies

Arranged by Andrew Belling

1. As I was out walk-ing one morn-ing for plea-sure, I
2. Ear-ly each spring we round up for the do-gies, We

spied a young cow-boy a - rid-ing a - long. His hat was thrown
mark 'em and brand 'em, and bob off their tails. We round up the

back and his spurs were a - jing-ling. And as he ap - proached he was
hors-es and pack up our sad-dles. Then off in the morn-ing to

sing-ing this song:
hit the long trail.

Whoop-ee ti - yi - yo, git a-

Chorus

26

long lit - tle do - gies. It's your mis - for - tune and none of my

own. Whoop - ee ti - yi - yo, git a - long lit - tle

do - gies. You know that Wy - o - ming will be your new home.

Sing Chorus of "Home on the Range"

Repeat Chorus of "Git Along Little Dogies" twice

Blow the Man Down

Arranged by Andrew Belling

2. After a while when the last whale is caught.
   Way! Hey! Blow the man down.
   All a man wants is his gal at home port.
   Give me some time to blow the man down.

3. When you've been at sea, boys, one sight sure is grand,…
   When the watch yells that he's just sighted land,…

4. Soon I'm a-walkin' down Paradise Street,…
   A pretty young maiden I happen to meet,…

5. Says she to me, "Sir, will you stand a treat?"…
   "Delighted," says I, "for a maiden so sweet."…

6. Blow the man down, boys, let's blow the man down,…
   There's nothin' as sweet as a maiden from town,…

28

The Doodles

Arranged by Andrew Belling

Two step

1. Oh, I went down South for to see my pal, sing - in' Pol - ly wol - ly doo - dle all the
2. Oh, my gal she is a maid - en fair, sing - in' Pol - ly wol - ly doo - dle all the

day. For my Pol - ly is a spunk - y gal sing - in'
with— laugh - ing eyes and curl - y hair sing - in'

Pol - ly wol - ly doo - dle all the day. *Chorus* Fare thee well, fare thee well, fare thee

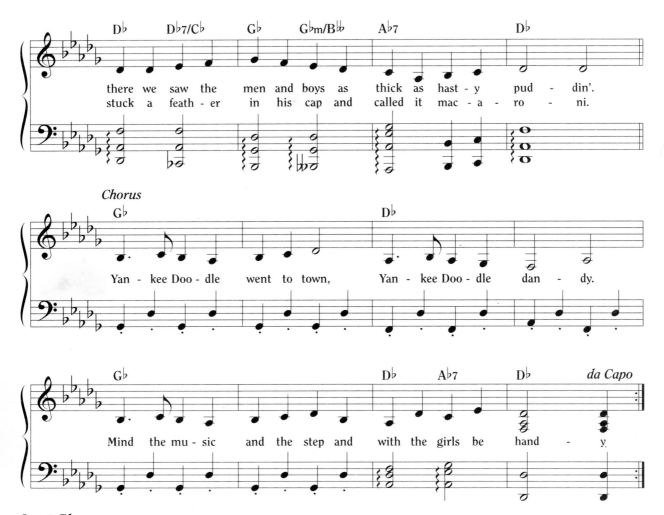

there we saw the men and boys as thick as hast-y pud - din'.
stuck a feath-er in his cap and called it mac - a - ro - ni.

Chorus

Yan - kee Doo - dle went to town, Yan - kee Doo - dle dan - dy.

Mind the mu - sic and the step and with the girls be hand - y.

da Capo

Last Chorus:

3. Yankee Doodle went to town, Yankee Doodle dandy.
   Yankee Doodle is my love,
   Singin' Polly wolly doodle all the day.